How to Organize for School-Based Management

John Prasch

Association for Supervision and Curriculum Development
Alexandria, Virginia

The Author

JOHN PRASCH is an Instructor in the Department of Educational Administration, University of Nebraska at Lincoln, and was formerly Superintendent of Schools in Lincoln, Nebraska, and Racine, Wisconsin.

Copyright© 1990 by the Association for Supervision and Curriculum Development, 1250 N. Pitt St., Alexandria, VA 22314.

Printed in the United States of America. Typeset on Xerox ™ Ventura Publisher 2.0. Printed by Automated Graphics Systems.

Ronald S. Brandt, *Executive Editor*
Nancy Modrak, *Managing Editor, Books*
Carolyn R. Pool, *Associate Editor*
Stephanie Kenworthy, *Assistant Manager, Production Services*
Valerie Sprague, *Desktop Typesetter*

$6.95
ASCD Stock No. 611-90093
ISBN 0-87120-174-7

Cataloging-In-Publication Data:

Prasch, John.
    How to organize for school-based management /
    by John Prasch.
    p. cm.
    Includes bibliographical references (p.).
    ISBN 0-87120–174-7 : $6.95
    1. School management and organization—United States.   I.
    Title
  LB2805. P74   1990
  371.2'00973—dc20
                                                90-43061
                                                   CIP

How to Organize for School-Based Management

Why School-Based Management?

DEMANDS TO RESTRUCTURE THE EDUCATIONAL SYSTEM CONTINUE to increase. Not yet exhausted by the frenzy of new policies, programs, and regulations most states spawned in the 1980s, the National Governors' Association adopted restructuring as its educational agenda for the 1990s (Cohen 1988). Governors are astute politicians; they do not stand alone. They are responding to a growing consensus calling for improvements in the efficiency and productivity of schools, in tune with massive restructuring in business, industry, and agriculture and with rapid demographic and social changes.

Much of the dialogue to date deals convincingly with the reasons for restructuring, but less precisely with how it is to come about. Restructuring means different things to different people, and the activities forwarded under its banner are many and diverse.

Nevertheless, imbedded in many of the approaches to restructuring is the concept of site-based (or school-based) management (SBM). SBM is consistent with, if not parallel to, other popular themes such as teacher empowerment and shared decision making. The concept fits industry's move toward decentralization and participatory management—the idea that decisions are better when made at operational points in the hierarchy. The statement by President Bush and the governors following the President's educational summit in 1989 lists decentralization of authority and decision making as one of the marks of successful restructuring (Pierce 1989). According to Ernest Boyer (1989), president of the Carnegie Foundation for the Advancement of Teaching, "In shaping a national strategy for education, school-based management is crucial."

1

U.S. Secretary of Education Lauro Cavazos coupled his theme of choice to SBM by saying, "Schools of choice must also have school-based management" (quoted in Snider 1989).

This book stems from the conviction that SBM is a part of the continuing restructuring movement and that educators need to know how to organize for its implementation. Educators may be understandably wary, having been criticized on the one hand for being impervious to change and accused, on the other, of jumping on every bandwagon. Yet they should rejoice at this turn away from the stifling regulatory nature of earlier reform measures and welcome the freedom to change that is implicit in the SBM rhetoric. SBM is grassroots restructuring, a bottom-up approach that depends on local adoption of reform ideas. SBM philosophy fits the considerable volume of educational literature on the change process, much of which has been ignored by noneducator policymakers. At last it may be recognized that teachers and school administrators know how to improve schools. But the pendulum swings. Seizing this opportunity requires practical expertise. From this point of view, a "how to" book is timely.

Rather than a cookbook, this is a guide for putting theory into practice. Intended to provide help in moving from lip service to action, it gives practical examples of ways to foster SBM, recognizing that the vast differences among school districts will create many alternative practices as the examples are applied. Though the mechanisms explained provide only samples of the variety of ways to proceed, the discussion of benefits, drawbacks, attitudes, and roles is generic to any plan.

By its nature, SBM rests on a commitment to situational management and leadership. That is, the dynamics of any given situation determine the most effective procedures; what works best in one place may not work elsewhere. It is inevitable and healthy that the degrees of implementation, the methods, and the results of SBM will vary.

Schools also have varying degrees of freedom when installing SBM, depending on state statutes and local circumstances controlling their operation. Empowering teachers to select textbooks, for example, may not be an option in states that make statewide adoptions. The regulatory controls under which schools operate, ranging from curriculum mandates to minimum salaries and including personnel credentialing and accreditation rules, vary widely from state to state. Even the best intentioned accrediting agencies limit the operational choices of individual schools. Despite these limits, there is a wide range of possibilities for implementation; practitioners need to choose those that are applicable or allowable in their own districts.

SBM is not new. It has been and is being practiced in varying degrees by school systems throughout the country. The American Association of School Administrators (1990), in its 1989-90 opinions and status of members survey, reported that almost one-fourth of the school districts represented had implemented SBM. An additional quarter had such a move under consideration. Although organizational emphasis on centralized authority is characteristic of many school districts, such practice cannot be documented as the norm. The ideals of democratic administration of schools are as old as programs to prepare administrators. The popularity of these concepts, now reborn or given new labels, simply means that school districts will move from where they are on the continuum to some further point. Viewing SBM in this light gives it sanity and perspective and identifies it as a rational change rather than a bandwagon move.

In deference to the flexibility inherent in SBM, I purposely avoid a tight definition of the term. It is more practical and more useful if allowed different meanings for different school districts. Renaming the movement to "school-centered decision making," as was done recently at a joint conference of the American Association of School Administrators, the National Education Association, the American Federation of Teachers, and the National Network for Educational Renewal (Fulbright 1989), is a legitimate attempt at a more precise definition. Yet the search for precision only plays semantic games with a concept whose very essence encourages variability.

Pros and Cons

If fueled by logic, the choice to install SBM implies a careful weighing of its advantages and disadvantages. Presumed advantages include:

• *Better programs for students.* Resources are more likely to match student needs when instructional decisions are made by those who work more directly with students.

• *Full use of human resources.* SBM recognizes the expertise and competencies of those to whom instruction is entrusted.

• *Higher quality decisions.* In an organization of highly trained individuals, joint decisions represent a pooling of expertise and ensure that issues are examined from a variety of viewpoints.

• *Increased staff loyalty and commitment.* The opportunity to participate develops a sense of ownership. Plans are more vigorously implemented by those who help make them.

• *Development of staff leadership skills.* Wider participation increases leadership opportunities for more individuals. Staff members build a broader understanding of the organization and have more opportunities to enlarge or change their roles.

• *Clear organizational goals.* Successful SBM depends on a careful balance between autonomy and control, which can only be achieved through full understanding of the organization's mission and goals.

• *Improved communication.* Wide participation in decisions requires full understanding of the issues and possession of all pertinent information.

• *Improved staff morale.* Staff members feel better about their organization and its leadership when they know their opinions are valued, sought, and used. This provides the opportunity to attract and retain higher quality personnel.

• *Support for staff creativity and innovation.* The flexibility SBM provides counterbalances organizational bureaucracy and frees staff to take risks.

• *Greater public confidence.* By allowing parents, constituents, and students a larger voice, SBM increases their understanding, responds more readily and accurately to their needs or demands, and increases their interest and support.

• *Enhanced fiscal accountability*. Staff members will manage more carefully the resources they actually control.

• *Restructuring*. Because SBM changes roles, responsibilities, and district organization, its implementation represents a restructuring. Paula White (1989) argues, "SBM is different from past decentralization efforts which merely shifted authority from a central board of education to smaller local boards."

Despite the current popularity of SBM, it has some disadvantages as well as implementation barriers. Knowing both in advance is helpful in smoothing the installation. Some disadvantages of SBM are:

• *More work*. Decision sharing at the site is time consuming, and staff members can ill afford to become enmeshed in costly discussion of trivial matters or be handicapped by excessive meetings or committee work. Upper level management of a site-based enterprise takes more time and effort because it is less routine, demands more coordination, and is generally more complex.

• *Less efficiency*. Monolithic, centralized organization appears to be more efficient in terms of per-unit dollar costs, expenditure of time, or straight-line, no-nonsense task accomplishment. Convincing a tax-conscious public that efficiency and effectiveness are not the same is, therefore, an added public relations burden of SBM.

• *Diluted benefits of specialization*. If knowledge is power, the in-depth knowledge of the specialist is a valuable commodity in an ever more specialized society. In a sense, SBM limits the decision-making authority of the central office specialist and moves it to the building-level generalist. A specialist, alone, may make more informed decisions than a group by virtue of greater expertise.

• *Uneven school performance*. Schools that are already weak will not automatically flourish when given more autonomy. Indeed, the very cause of the weakness may be that local leadership is unable to capitalize on additional freedom. By contrast, strong schools with alert staffs are likely to become stronger under SBM. The potential differences among schools in scope and sequence of curriculum place a hardship on students forced to transfer schools.

• *Greater need for staff development.* Staffs need help in assuming the new roles that SBM requires. Moreover, to fully capitalize on the advantages of SBM, staff members need continuous access to new knowledge and skills. Retraining—as well as initial training—is a continuous need.

• *Possible confusion about new roles and responsibilities.* The development of new roles and relationships inevitably creates a messy period, loaded with risks of misunderstanding, and having potential for personal insecurity and eventual feuding among staff members.

• *Coordination difficulties.* Autonomous sites may pursue their self-interest in disregard of the goals of the total institution. Conflict is possible between advocates of the individual school and advocates of the higher, general good. SBM can establish power struggles among administrators, teachers, parents, and students. Negotiating the inevitable conflicts is a difficult managerial task.

• *Unintended consequences.* If the authority to act and the resources to implement are not provided to site-based staffs when their participation is invited, alienation results. Conditioned by previous swings of the pendulum of reform, teachers are perceptive when judging if actions match rhetoric. The best intentioned changes run the risk of damaging the fragile network of trust. Staff members will always check external public relations against internal reality. In the loosely structured school world, opportunities abound for co-option, symbolic response, and noncompliance.

• *Irreversible shifts.* Once the process is started, it is difficult and traumatic to change directions.

Some barriers to installation of SBM are:

• *Resistance to change.* Preserving the status quo is frequently the line of least resistance and provides staff members with the greatest degree of comfort.

• *Unstable school leadership.* The change in membership of boards of education is institutionalized through the election process. Superintendents and principals often change positions.

• *Budget increases*. Change that costs money is difficult to promote in the cost-conscious educational environment. Both installation and maintenance of SBM require additional staff development funding.

• *Existing governance structures*. Schools are imprisoned by a surprising range of federal and state laws and regulations as well as by the policies of local boards of education. Moreover, union contracts frequently restrict the roles and functions of members.

• *Misinterpretation of control*. Striking the appropriate balance between centralized and decentralized control—and making sure that that balance is fully understood by all staff members—is difficult.

• *"Quick-fix" attitude*. SBM's installation will take time, and its results may not be immediately identified. Since SBM will be no panacea, current hype may set expectations too high.

• *Inappropriate staffing*. There is a danger that central office or administrative staff will be inappropriately reduced if the complexity of implementation is underestimated or if the reasons for installing SBM go beyond the purpose of improving learning for students.

Reduction of administrative staff, a common goal in many reform initiatives, is not a goal of SBM. Changing administrative roles is an objective, one that may or may not be related to staff size.

Not all the moves to SBM are the result of logical analysis of its pros and cons. It is possible to be swept into SBM by the momentum of its popularity simply because it's the thing to do. Some features of SBM, most notably the establishment of parent councils, have been legislated in at least three states. The rhetoric of the movement is seductive.

Strange as it may seem for a concept that celebrates cooperation, some school districts are pushed into SBM via the collective bargaining table. SBM entered into as the result of a win-lose power struggle may well founder. If begun under a cloud of coercion or if perceived as the opening battle in a continuing war, activities that implement SBM can be unproductive and impermanent. Trust is critical to the successful implementation of SBM.

The Importance of Attitudes

Those who would successfully implement SBM must embrace a state of mind that includes the following principles:

• SBM advocates understand that in democratic environments power is achieved by giving it away rather than by struggling for more. SBM flourishes when power is freely and cheerfully shared. Such environments thrive only when there are attitudes of trust in the ability of colleagues and trust that their motives are consistent with organizational goals.

• Successful implementation of SBM requires understanding and acceptance on the part of all staff that the essential mission of schooling—the instruction of students—occurs in the classroom, and that all other activities of the district exist only to support that instruction. The most telling evaluation of SBM will, in the long run, rest on the question of improved student achievement.

• In the SBM environment, personnel are not supervised in the sense that there are ordinate and subordinate positions. Staff do not "report to" but rather "work with" their colleagues. The hierarchical organizational chart may be a necessary bureaucratic appendage, but not one to be taken too seriously. Individuals feel that their contributions are valued and that they are free to take risks.

• Accountability is achieved through a process of goal setting with a maximum of freedom provided staff regarding how goals are met. Problem solving is accomplished by teams, and evaluation focuses on programs, not on individuals.

• Diversity and disagreement are revered and are perceived as opportunities for learning rather than symptoms of discord and divisiveness.

• Although maintaining positive human relations remains important, successful SBM requires key staff members to be oriented more to the organization as a whole. Emphasis on the success of schools suggests a departure from the behavioral norms that fit the non-integrative organization, as described by Woodward (1958) and Wieck (1976). In SBM, teachers get as much satisfaction from the school's success as from their individual accomplishments. The congruence of personal and institutional goals is a sign of organizational good health.

• Larry Dlugosh, Superintendent of Schools in Grand Island, Nebraska, speaking at the annual convocation of Nebraska School Administrators in August 1989, summarized the orientation necessary for a successful SBM plan as "goal driven, needs responsive, results oriented, and teamwork/group operationalized."

Planning Decisions

Several preliminary planning decisions need to be made in picking an implementation path for SBM. Installation procedures will be different for an evolution as opposed to a revolution. Also, it may be a good idea to determine in advance how far along the SBM continuum a district wants to go.

An obvious way to move into SBM is slowly, one step at a time. An important advantage of the incremental approach is the time it provides for careful training of staff at each stage of implementation. Time is also helpful in giving staff members a more comfortable climate in which to adjust to change. Districts that already have some elements of SBM in place can simply add additional elements. Finally, the evolutionary path fits a quieter process when a low rather that a high profile is desirable. According to Leonard Burns and Jeanne Howes (1988), in their description of the Parkway, Missouri, SBM plan, "significant and lasting improvement takes considerable time."

Although common sense suggests a slower pace, circumstances often argue strongly for more precipitous action. High-profile, fast-paced action is more likely to generate enthusiasm, full involvement, and commitment from staff, as well as public support. Rapid change may be necessary to make full use of SBM's newfound popularity. Programs mandated by legislated action or born of negotiated agreements may not provide for leisurely implementation. For example, the new Chicago plan, an extreme form of SBM with 540 local school councils mandated by state legislative action, was put in place in a year's time.

If forced into a fast track, a district should use the circumstance as a positive opportunity for change. At this point, if the changes are to be substantive and lasting, leaders must be especially sensitive to the human factors involved in change and understand the inherent pitfalls in SBM.

Related to the pacing decision is the question of whether to begin with pilot schools or include all schools at the same time. The philosophy of SBM suggests that it might be best to proceed on a broken front with all schools in the district participating but at varying stages of implementation. Selecting pilot schools implies special attention to some sites and may, in the long run, destroy the climate conducive to successful total implementation. Using pilot schools creates a "project" mentality, suggesting an experiment or trial rather than a permanent management improvement. Pilots or projects also connote the development of a model, whereas SBM should anticipate each school's developing its own response. SBM philosophy is reinforced when the installation strategy creates the enabling mechanisms and encourages their use by all schools in a nonprescriptive way.

Nevertheless, many districts, especially larger ones, choose the pilot school approach. Hanson and Marburger (1988), who recommend the pilot, report that St. Louis started SBM with 12 schools out of 116 and added another 12 the next year. Allentown, Pennsylvania, started with 4 of 20 schools, and Dade County, Florida, started with 33 of 260. Ann Bradley (1990) describes the process by which New York City schools request to be included in their program. About 100 of 1,100 are expected to be chosen to participate in the first year.

Rather than arguing the relative merits of one type of action over the other, it is important to emphasize that a conscious decision on pacing is part of the installation plan. Also, an early decision on how far to carry SBM is important because it affects all aspects of the plan, including the pacing and sequencing as well as the amounts and kinds of staff development needed. Effective SBM is not synonymous with complete decentralization of all functions. Moreover, the centralization vs. decentralization issue is not a matter of either/or but of finding the proper balance. In practical terms, the task is to identify functions that are best performed when centralized and to centralize only those.

In school settings, for example, it makes sense to centralize the purchasing function. Teachers can ill afford the time needed individually to buy paper, pencils, and instructional supplies. Accordingly, writing the specifications, taking the bids, checking the invoices, ensuring the delivery, and making the necessary accounting entries are all functions best centralized. Nevertheless, teachers can still help decide what kind of pencils to purchase. Although teachers may not write specifications, they should influence the purchasing process because they are in the best position to know what's needed. This is a good illustration of the balance between centralized and decentralized functions and also supports the concept that the central office exists only to serve the school.

Student transportation is another function best centralized. Buying and maintaining school buses, developing efficient routes, and hiring and training drivers are all activities better done on a districtwide basis. The required balance is maintained as long as the transportation system is seen solely as a service supporting instruction. When requirements of the busing schedule interfere with the delivery of instruction, it's time to involve building-based staff in the scheduling decisions.

Payroll, legal services, and food services are also best centralized. Centralization provides efficiency and cost effectiveness and becomes most useful when there is a high need for coordination. The concept of SBM is well served when site-based staff are not unnecessarily saddled with functions more effectively performed at a central level.

Start with the
Board of Education

DESPITE THE CURRENT PUBLIC ENTHUSIASM, FULL AND CONTINUING
support for SBM from members of the board of education
may be one of the more difficult hurdles. Although likely to
give lip service to SBM, most members of boards of
education are more comfortable with conventional
management models. They understand bureaucratic
arrangements, they believe they were elected to control,
they favor tight over loose organizational modes, and they
overestimate the extent to which their decisions affect
classroom behavior.

Because of the responsibility they feel to their
constituents, board members are frightened of losing
control, particularly if differences between buildings are
perceived as chaotic or permissive. The responsibility to
explain things to the public causes board members to favor
simple, easy-to-understand organization. Effective SBM
produces success stories at individual schools, but typical
board-member reaction to success at one building is to
mandate the procedure districtwide.

Moreover, the task of keeping the board in tune is a
continuing one. Elections change board membership, and
newcomers frequently campaign on a platform of bringing
about change, if only for its own sake. Given the long time
span necessary from successful installation and
implementation to noticeable results, continuity of
leadership is a critical factor.

Nevertheless, board commitment is of paramount
importance because SBM can succeed only when the
policies of the district support its philosophy. James
Mitchell (1990), Superintendent of School District #2,
Northglen, Colorado, says, "Most of the policies in the

policy manual reflect centralized control." It is through the development and adoption of policy statements that SBM becomes legitimized and institutionalized. Examples of useful policy statements are presented in the chapter of this book entitled "Build Implementing Mechanisms."

Several can be used to get board commitment and maintain the SBM philosophy.

Hold Board Retreats

The in-depth discussion of philosophy needed for board members to develop attitudes associated with SBM requires a format different from routine business meetings. A daylong retreat, away from the usual meeting place and free of disturbances, can afford a more appropriate setting. Use of an outside facilitator often enhances productivity. Retreats, institutionalized as an annual event, provide an excellent vehicle for establishing goals for the district, a necessity in SBM. Retreats are also a good way to orient new board members.

Hold Work Sessions

Short of a full retreat, informal work sessions are helpful in the SBM installation process. Such meetings are particularly useful for the extended discussions needed for policy development. Because finding sufficient time for policy debate is a persistent problem for many boards, having a specific vehicle for such work is a convenient solution. Retreats and work sessions are also better environments than regular meetings for discussing and evaluating the role of the board in the SBM program.

Target the Dialogue

While the advantage of retreats and work sessions is the additional time not usually available at regular business meetings, the availability of time is also an invitation for discussion to wander. A tightly drawn agenda and carefully planned process control are essential for a productive session. Though controlled, the agenda must still provide for broad coverage and free-wheeling opinion on basic philosophic issues. Indeed, the philosophic nature of SBM demands careful organization to reach consensus or closure.

A sample agenda might address the following questions:

- What are the reasons for changing?
- What purposes will change serve?
- How do educational institutions change? (This question provides an excellent opportunity to share with board members the educator's perspective on the nature of organizations and the change process.)
- How do board members best facilitate change?
- What are the next steps? Who does what?

Get Reports from Individual Schools

SBM is greatly enhanced if time is allotted on the agenda of each board meeting for reports from individual schools. Staff members or constituents should actively participate in the reports so that board members learn that buildings and their staffs differ, having their own personalities, strengths, and needs.

Disaggregate the Database

Strong support for SBM is shown by disaggregating, or separating out, school-supplied information to emphasize the differences among schools. When only districtwide data are shown, the implication is that all schools are alike.

Moreover, there are sound statistical reasons for disaggregating data. Aggregate test scores, for example, easily mask both strengths and weaknesses of individual schools and obscure information that may be much more useful for diagnostic analysis or for guiding programs of improvement.

The practical problems associated with unfair comparisons among buildings, resulting from disaggregated achievement data, must be met head on. The antidote is to supply copious additional information describing environmental circumstances, from one building to another, and to mount public information programs to assist in the appropriate interpretation of achievement information. Indeed, a frank examination of the issues surrounding comparisons makes a strong case for SBM as the best method to ensure that programs fit the clients.

Plan Strategically

The principles of strategic planning support and enhance the ideas of SBM. The emphasis on an environmental scan, a visionary mission statement, and a clear set of goals establishes an important backdrop for the coordination of building-level activities. At the same time, the development of action plans to accomplish goals serves to give buildings an appropriate site-based role. The Richardson (Texas) Independent School District, for example, started its SBM effort with a mission statement and strategic plan (Carr 1988).

Emphasize Board Functions

Board members need reinforcement and instruction if they are to play their roles properly. One direct strategy to accomplish this is careful control of the agenda. Periodic evaluation of board functioning also helps. Use of experienced outside facilitators as process observers, along with careful follow-up on recommendations, helps keep the board on track.

Service on a board of education can become stressful and frustrating, but the organization and emphasis of board work can go a long way toward substituting fulfillment for frustration. For example, there is great satisfaction in planning when it produces results, in setting goals when horizons are elevated, and in establishing policies when they energize staff.

Make Comparisons with Business

Many board members are prone to want schools to be more businesslike. Current trends in business and industry strongly support the principles of SBM. When the board is fully committed, a broad-based development committee can help create awareness throughout the system and assist with the decisions about pacing, sequencing, and the depth of the SBM program. Such a committee can also serve the ongoing functions of monitoring, evaluating, and adjusting the SBM plan as it is installed.

Define New Leadership Roles

THIS CHAPTER ILLUSTRATES DESIRED ROLE CHANGES FOR EACH classification of personnel, which will help ensure the successful installation of SBM.

The Board of Education

Although ultimate control of the district rests with the board of education, SBM requires the board to change the way it exercises that control. Instead of taking direct administrative action, it must set policy, establish goals, and monitor results. Instead of leading by exhortation and demand, it must lead by enunciating a visionary mission statement and by setting goals that stretch the abilities of the staff. The board must abandon the role of establishing rules for standardization and uniformity and accept a coordinating role played out by monitoring results rather than processes. Board members must understand that SBM does not change the legal governance system of schools and, more important, that they do not give up authority by sharing decisions. But in discharging its responsibility for accountability, the board changes from an inspectorial role to providing a forum for the staff to report progress on goals.

Board members need guidance in learning to accept a role on the higher ground and to delegate in ways that best use staff talents. Mundane as it may sound, helping board members handle telephone complaints is a staff function that contributes to the ability of a board to play its appropriate role in SBM. Without staff guidance, board members are easily trapped into spending their time on relatively trivial matters instead of the larger issues. The often fuzzy demarcation between policy development and administration becomes more clear as SBM is implemented.

The board must also accept a public relations role in celebrating the diversity among its schools and in championing the right of school sites to be different. Board policy must define roles and must be explicit with regard to the power and authority to be delegated and shared with parent councils and school staff.

The Superintendent

All of the items covered in the "Importance of Attitudes" section could be repeated at this point because they apply most directly to the superintendent's role. In addition to changing his own attitudes, however, the superintendent must clearly understand that sharing power in no way relieves him of the burden of leadership. Leadership of the highest order is required to convince a board of education to adopt the necessary policies and the operational style required of SBM, especially considering that the superintendent serves in a subordinate position to the board. Likewise, the superintendent must initiate all the practices and make available all the staff development activities that support SBM, yet he must accomplish this task in a nondirective way. The staff must not only be persuaded to accept the idea in theory but must also be enticed into active participation.

Clearly, SBM demands stronger, not weaker, leadership of the superintendent and requires a style of leadership more complicated and difficult. The "command and control" approach gives way to a "beseech and facilitate" mode. The superintendent must abandon the "take charge" style for one that encourages and supports others to take charge. In this respect, the superintendent becomes less the super-administrator who manages programs on some grand scheme and more the mentor who, behind the scenes, helps people grow. Rather than the person who always has the final answer, the superintendent must have the key questions—he must be less a talker, more a listener. The SBM superintendent makes heroes rather than becoming one. Murphy (1989) sums it up by saying, "Superintendents need to pay more attention to the unheroic dimensions of leadership if they are to promote local autonomy." Thus, the emerging concept of "leader as servant" fits the SBM philosophy.

Although restricted to a softer leadership style, the superintendent must nevertheless transmit an overall, inspirational vision of mission to the entire organization. Such a vision is extremely important to SBM because it provides the glue that holds the organization together. The task is accomplished not by making pronouncements but by engaging the staff in conversations that help them work together to develop and accept consensus. Such work depends on establishing the institutional climate for collegial work and skill in group dynamics.

Conflict management becomes an important skill for SBM superintendents because the process of sharing decisions is likely to produce conflict. The superintendent must not view conflict as dysfunctional but, to preserve its productivity, must learn to mediate conflicts rather than resolve them by decree.

SBM is enhanced if the superintendent can abandon an adversarial role with employee unions in favor of a stance that makes union officials partners in the installation effort. Establishing such a relationship is a year-round activity, requiring special attention to the problems related to the negotiating season. Collaborative work on SBM outside of negotiation time prevents it from becoming a bargaining chip.

Central Office Staff Members

Depending on the size of the district, a varying number of central office staff members hold assorted titles and perform more or less specialized functions. To get each of them to play a role consistent with the tenets of SBM often requires a significant role change, sometimes both difficult and traumatic. The important shift is from power by virtue of title to power based solely on ability to serve. Leaders must challenge the idea that all important functions are necessarily based in the central office. That is not to suggest that functions be eliminated, but only that they be relocated. The following more specific observations refer to staff titles commonly found in school district central office organizations.

Subject-Matter Specialists

If SBM is to work, those who serve at the central office as specialists in a subject, such as mathematics or reading, must give up any vestige of control and assume the role of facilitator or helper. Giving up control means among other things, that they do not have a portion of the school's budget to manage, nor are they expected to evaluate the performance of school-based teachers. A change in title from "supervisor" or "director" to "consultant" can convey the direction of the intended change. Assuming the changed role, however, is more difficult than merely changing the name. The best way for specialists to play their new role is to work with individual schools on an on-call basis. Specialists must be convinced that they are more effective when their services are sought rather than imposed—not an unreasonable assumption. Since the frequency with which they are called is a measure of perceived expertise or need, the role is challenging. Yet, as in other aspects of SBM, such working conditions are powerful motives to hone staff capabilities.

The possibility that the services of specialists might be purchased by schools on an ad hoc basis, rather than being provided by permanent central office staff, is a legitimate issue in the move to SBM.

The Business Manager

Most school districts have a business manager who occupies a relatively high rung on the organizational ladder. Given the increased complexity and cost of operating schools, the business function takes on increased importance. The general perception is that money controls. Unfortunately, a mismatch usually exists between available funds and the tasks facing education. By nature, business operations are concerned with direct and logical manipulations of objects and money—actions that fit an autocratic management style. Also, functions most likely to be centralized are usually assigned to the business manager.

For all of these reasons, the business manager, more than any other central office administrator, tends to gather power and have the most difficulty playing the power-sharing role required in SBM.

The business manager must change from the role of a money manager to that of an educator, one as dedicated to the instruction of students as any employee in the district. She can no longer ignore the meetings that deal with instruction, but must participate in enough of them to understand the instructional mission and to be viewed as knowledgeable and supportive. The business manager must be concerned less with efficiency and more with effectiveness. She must relinquish sole proprietorship of fiscal data and assume responsibility for sharing such data and presenting them in a fashion that all can understand. Instead of being the stern protector of district funds with a ready negative response to every request, the business manager must play the role of enabler, helping site managers stretch their dollar resources. Granted, this is a difficult role change, but it gives the business manager a chance to change from a "bad guy" to a "good guy."

The Personnel Director

The personnel officer must give up the power base of being the final selector of staff and play a role that facilitates sound selections by others. As with subject-matter specialists, a name change that drops the title of "director" may be helpful in announcing the change. "Human resources manager" or "personnel manager" may more accurately describe this function in an SBM district. In any event, this person selects and interviews less, but ensures better selection and interviewing procedures throughout the district. He keeps a comprehensive personnel database that includes information on active applicants, current vacancies, professional information on all staff members, results of exit interviews, and current research on all phases of personnel management, particularly the best methods for staff evaluation and counseling. By improving procedures and developing a list of qualified applicants, the human resources manager exercises a powerful quality control function while allowing site managers ultimate control over selection.

Instead of merely hiring and assigning people, the personnel manager facilitates a broad-based program of improving staff relations through such activities as administering the benefits program, assisting in handling grievances and other aspects of the union contract, and keeping key staff members informed on improved human relations skills. In this sense, the personnel manager, like the superintendent, becomes a developer of people.

The Special Education Director

Many school districts have a central office specialist who directs a program of services for handicapped or special needs students. Frequently, teachers who work in more than one school report to the central office director of such a program. In SBM, special education directors and teachers must change their points of reference so that the roles they play work to integrate their program into the school's regular program, as directed by that school's principal. Although such arrangements complicate scheduling and other aspects of special education, their long-term benefits are worth the effort. In fact, they may be the only avenue for achieving the integration implied in mainstreaming.

The Principal

Although it may appear that in SBM authority and responsibility for the local school have been delegated to the principal, that is not a completely accurate reading of how SBM works. True, the principalship becomes an important focal point, but SBM provides the principal with much more powerful tools for successful operation of the school.

At the outset, the principal, like the superintendent, must enter the SBM arena with all the necessary attitudes for successful installation. With the right mental set, the principal has the help and cooperation of the entire school staff in the management of the school. Not only is the principal empowered by a different and more effective staff support system, but she now has available the full range of central office services, on her terms. Whereas the role of the principal has always been to orchestrate the services of various providers to create optimal educational experiences for students, under SBM the principal has added authority and freedom to get the job done. This is a welcome reversal of a longstanding trend to erode the principal's role by the onslaughts of increased central office control; aggressive union intrusion; and new state, federal, and judicial regulations. Reversal of this trend is in accord with the research on effective schools, which emphasizes the importance of the principalship.

The principal must expand her horizons to play this new role. No longer can she hide behind the policy handbook or central office regulations to defend her decisions. Since the central office cannot be used as a scapegoat, the principal must play a more directly accountable role with staff and constituents. Rather than viewing the central office staff as enemies, the SBM principal sees them as resources and frequently seeks and welcomes their help.

To fully exploit her new authority and freedom, the principal needs to sharpen her human relations skills to attract the meaningful involvement of staff and constituents. She must be a master in group dynamics so that meetings are productive. The SBM principal must abandon the routine tasks of keeping school and embrace the more important task of creating a climate in which all staff and students share responsibility for not just keeping school, but also for improving its effectiveness. Instead of being the disciplinarian for the institution, the principal sets a tone in which staff and students share responsibility for behavior, and the frequency of problems diminishes.

In SBM, the principal has an expanded role in the community that the school serves. No longer can she be solely concerned about the school; she must get to know the community it serves much more intimately. The principal must analyze the peculiar needs of the community and fashion a school program responsive to those needs. Most likely, the SBM plan will include a parent council, which creates a new relationship between the principal and the constituents. This new role requires more listening and more questioning than the principal's traditional relationship with parent groups. Indeed, in the Chicago plan, school councils hire and fire principals. William Snider (1990) reports that 49 principals were ousted by the votes of newly formed local school councils.

In discharging responsibilities for staff supervision, the principal departs from the role of overseer of each faculty member. Instead, she adopts a "management by exception" mode, playing the supervisory role only with the small percentage of staff members whose performance is marginal, and working with the rest of the staff as an equal partner in the search for more effective instructional techniques.

A key to effective power sharing is information sharing. Staff must have access to relevant information if they are to participate intelligently in decision making. No longer can the principal's office be simply the repository of information; the principal must play an aggressive role in disseminating the information. This responsibility includes finding ways to package and store information for easy access and use.

The SBM principal assumes a new relationship with noncertified staff, such as custodians and food service workers. In the SBM environment, these workers are more a part of the building staff and less under the direction of the central office. They must be welcomed and helped to become a part of the decision-making process at the building, when appropriate. The individuals lowest on the table of organization can make significant contributions when the decisions affect their work.

In short, the principal's new role is to find ways to empower all staff members to maximize their contributions in successfully attaining the school's goals.

Teachers

The teacher empowerment rhetoric that is part of the SBM movement is easily misinterpreted. Teachers must be empowered to do what they do best, which is to teach students. Empowering teachers to be administrators does not necessarily move a school toward its goals, is not welcomed by most teachers, and is unnecessary if administrators do their jobs properly. SBM implies that teachers must be served or ministered to by their principals and superintendents so that students have better learning opportunities. Time for teachers to teach must be protected. Teachers are empowered when they can act as, and are treated as, professionals.

Nevertheless, SBM changes teachers' roles by demanding more of their attention to policy and procedural matters. Teachers, therefore, need to become more adept in group dynamics so their dialogue can be more productive and less time-consuming. More important, if teachers are to become significant participants in decision making, they need to be better informed, more alert to the large-scale issues affecting all schools, and, most of all, abreast of research results regarding the improvement of instruction. SBM challenges teachers to show that their new-found freedom can produce better results for students. Given the opportunity to take risks, teachers must become risk takers.

Any discussion of the teachers' role in SBM must recognize that the growth of auxiliary or support staff, such as counselors, psychologists, and special educators, has contributed to the loss of teacher power, at least to the extent that specialized personnel narrow the range and type of decisions reserved for teachers. Organizationally, support staff are often paid more, have greater control over their time, and are accorded more deference than are teachers. SBM must define these roles with care to ensure the primacy of teaching and to convince teachers that support staff are a resource *for teachers*. The inservice message is that teachers need training in the use of personnel resources, and the organizational implication is the need for team building.

SBM cannot flourish in a "we vs. they" environment. Teachers must therefore give up an adversarial relationship with administrators in the implementation of SBM. Fortunately, if administrators play their SBM roles properly, problems of adversarial relationships will diminish.

Parents

Parents, too, have new roles in SBM. If the movement is to be successful and if parents are to be involved, they must shift from the narrow concern, "What's good for my child?" to the broader concern, "What's good for all children?" This is a difficult shift, but with the establishment of powerful school-based parent councils, the success or demise of SBM depends on whether parents play a more selfless role. Unfortunately, history is replete with examples of how local-based power, when used for self-interest, forces a retreat to centralized control. For example, when local officials failed to address problems of racial and gender discrimination and lack of opportunity for limited-English-speaking students and handicapped children, the federal government felt compelled to act.

Parent councils must be guided around the rivalries and factions within the school. Moreover, although formed for the specific purpose of promoting the welfare of a given school, their activities should not be at the expense or detriment of other schools in the district.

The opportunity for greater parent involvement carries with it a responsibility for parents to be well informed on educational issues. As with staff members, SBM requires a greater time commitment of parents.

Fewer parents today have a direct relationship with schools because of demographic changes associated with lower birth rates, greater longevity, and employment outside the home. Also, the current emphasis on school partnerships with business creates more nonparent involvement with schools. These and other reasons argue for having nonparent constituents on site-based councils.

Build Implementing Mechanisms

ALL OF THE DISCUSSION OF ATTITUDES AND ALL THE STAFF. development activities for new roles are just a part of the nice-sounding talk about SBM. The crux of implementation is in the specific mechanisms that, when put in place, make SBM workable.

Getting Organized

Official policy statements adopted by the board clearly establish the tone for SBM. Policy statements are most useful when stated simply and in general terms. If SBM is to have any real meaning, schools and their staffs must have wide freedom within broad guidelines. This requirement translates to slimmed down policy manuals. Although their essence is clarity, overly detailed and prescriptive statements do not fit the SBM philosophy. Administrative regulations are developed to follow up or implement broad policies and tend, therefore, to be more focused.

Sample Policy 1

The Pleasant Valley School District is operated on an organizational plan in which the operational line of authority flows from the superintendent of schools directly to building principals and then, for instructional purposes, to teachers.

Sample Policy 2

The Pleasant Valley School District's Table of Organization shall clearly show the lines of authority for the operation of schools and shall indicate that all other functions support these operational lines.

Figure 1 shows a sample table of organization. Note that, in the figure, some personnel titles are shown in boxes while others are shown in bubbles. Also, there are direct lines between boxes that clearly trace the lines of authority, whereas the arrows from the bubbles show only direction, indicating to whom services flow but making no direct connection. Thus, the table of organization emphasizes line and staff distinctions and clearly implies an SBM approach, whereas conventional models usually suggest a more controlling function for many central office staff members.

FIGURE 1
SAMPLE TABLE OF ORGANIZATION

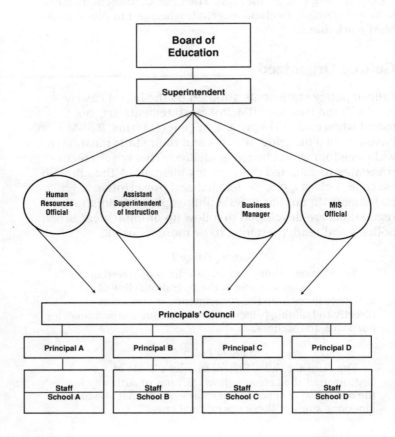

Note: MIS = Management Information System

Obviously, there can be many alternative patterns for tables of organization, and these patterns will vary with district size. The table presented in Figure 1 is intended to emphasize that, if the district intends to use SBM, the organizational chart must clearly show that buildings are in a direct line of authority with a minimum of intermediate decision makers.

An organizational structure in which principals report directly to the superintendent greatly enhances SBM. Such an arrangement reduces bureaucracy by providing the shortest possible vertical hierarchy, and it elevates the role of the principal to the leadership level required by SBM.

Superintendents of larger districts will protest that having all principals report to them creates an impossible management situation. They will point out a serious violation of accepted span-of-control concepts. Yet imposing central office positions between the principal and the superintendent is a sure way to minimize the site-based leadership role. Moreover, span-of-control worries are associated with tight supervisory models that connote ordinate-subordinate relationships antithetical to the collegiality and empowerment that SBM promises. Dealing directly with principals requires the superintendent to shift priorities; It also forces the superintendent to know the strengths and weaknesses of each principal and, more important, to develop a more thorough and accurate understanding of needs of the district.

Sample Regulation 2.1. A principals' council, to include all principals, will meet regularly with the superintendent. The purpose of the council is to advise the superintendent, to provide a forum for the identification and solution of district problems, and to exchange information.

The formal organization of a principals' council helps to alleviate the problems associated with having a large number of principals reporting directly to the superintendent. But it does a great deal more than that. Combining the expertise of the district's operational leadership creates an unexcelled sounding board for the review of all district policies and regulations. The council inevitably becomes a coordinating agency for the district, since it has representation from each site by someone who understands the program at that site and how district actions affect it. The council also serves as an important vehicle for the dissemination of ideas from one building to another, thus providing the cross-fertilization that spurs innovation. Information exchange through regular council meetings ensures common understandings among all line staff. It is significant that these advantages accrue not simply by having the principals together but by assembling them as site managers.

Principals are empowered through their participation on the council when they discover the effects of their deliberations on district progress. The council offers a window through which to see the district as a whole, which helps principals put their own work in perspective and counteracts the risk of myopia inherent in exclusive loyalty to a single site. Participation in the council is an avenue of professional growth as well as a convenient induction mechanism for beginners.

A corollary to the rule of having principals report to the superintendent is severely limiting the number of central office staff who do so. Decreasing the number of central office staff members who report directly to the superintendent clarifies that educators in these roles support, not direct, the instructional program. Consistent with this organizational concept, assistant principals are not members of the principal's council.

Although variations to the structure of a principals' council (or similar organization with a different title) are to be expected, the concept that site-based managers themselves are a team is key. Such a team helps maintain the balance between district and school goals and ensures that site programs advance the mission of the district as well as that of the school.

Sample Policy 3

School buildings in the Peaceful Valley School District are operationally under the control of the building principal. Principals have charge of and are responsible for the building and grounds, all supplies and equipment housed there, all students and staff assigned to the building, and all school-related activities carried on at the building.

It is important both that the extent of the site manager's responsibility be specified unequivocally in policy, and that the policy give the entire responsibility to the principal. However, the principal should have the flexibility to have parts of some functions delegated elsewhere.

For example, principals who want to maximize the time they spend on instructional matters may want to minimize the time they spend on managing custodial service in the building. When this is the case, they may request a central office person to draft the cleaning schedule, determine working hours, or even select the custodians. Providing for delegation of these services at the request of the principal, however, is completely different from centralizing this function by someone else's choice. When the site manager requests service, the implication is that the request can be withdrawn or the arrangement changed, and that control remains with the principal.

Furthermore, in SBM the arrangements for this service may vary from one school to the next. The loss in efficiency as seen from the central office point of view is balanced by the gain in effectiveness at the building level in terms of the service matching building needs.

Management of food services, supervision of special teachers who work in several buildings, and relationships with school nurses are other examples of building operations that raise questions of control. Deciding issues of this kind makes the principals' council most valuable. It may well be that the principal's council will agree that food services are most efficiently and effectively provided when centralized and delivered uniformly throughout the district. When the decision is made by the council, it is most likely to have strong support in the buildings.

Organizational policies and procedures, in addition to bestowing authority on the principal, must provide guidance on how that authority is used. The advantages of SBM are not realized by empowering principals unless they in turn empower their staffs.

Sample Policy 4

Building principals are required to manage their buildings by procedures that ensure staff and constituent participation.

Sample Regulation 4.1. The annual principal's report will describe the mechanisms that ensure staff participation.

Sample Regulation 4.2. Principals are required to have in place a written organizational plan that ensures the opportunity of constituent participation in the affairs of the school.

Parent councils at the building level are the centerpiece of many recently acclaimed SBM plans. Presumably, the difference between SBM parent councils and the more traditional PTAs or advisory committees is the degree to which the councils are given a formal role in decision making. Including parents, constituents, or students in the decision process is a logical and desirable extension of SBM, but exact arrangements will vary from one school community to the next. How council members are selected, how many there should be, how often they should meet, and what their agendas should be are all issues to be addressed when councils are formed. The critically important concern is for everyone involved to be completely clear on how the councils are to function. The following guidelines will help produce this clarity:

- Develop a clear statement of purpose.
- Accurately define the limits of authority, carefully delineating differences between advising, deciding, reviewing, and vetoing.
- Formalize a selection process that provides broad-based representation.
- Identify the kinds of issues with which the council will deal.
- Develop a clear understanding of the relationship of the council to the board of education, the superintendent, and the principal. Councils are not miniature school boards.
- Describe the relationship of the council with existing parent groups, such as special education advisory boards, school booster clubs, federal Chapter 1 advisory councils, and the PTA.
- Provide a formal and carefully structured orientation for all incoming council members.

SBM councils are sometimes made up of combinations of staff, parent, and student representatives. Marburger

(1985) prescribes which groups are to be represented "if it is to be called an SBM council." His material implies that the formation of a site-based management council, including parents, is a first step when installing SBM.

Setting Goals

If SBM is to produce better outcomes for students—its ultimate mission—then it must be goal-driven. At the district level, a statement of mission and of broad goals is an indispensable mechanism for keeping the centrifugal forces of SBM from tearing the institution apart. Objectives must also be written at the building level to describe how the building will further the mission and goals of the district. Attention to goals is the ultimate discipline by which buildings are freed to apply their methods.

Not only do a mission statement and a set of goals set the stage for productive teamwork, but when properly conceived, also help define the role of the board as it relates to the roles of central office staff and building personnel. Accepting tight definitions of the terms *mission*, *goals*, and *objectives*, rather than using them interchangeably, establishes a hierarchy among the terms.

In this hierarchy, mission is a single, visionary, timeless statement of purposed expressed in a way that inspires staff to rally around the cause. Goals, by contrast, define areas of emphasis (for a given period of time) intended to fulfill the mission. Objectives are achievable, measurable, time-bound, specific actions to accomplish goals. Within this hierarchy, framing the mission statement and prioritizing goals are board functions; setting objectives and developing action plans become building functions.

The current widespread emphasis on strategic planning in all public institutions provides many useful models for developing mission statements and setting goals. Workshops, training sessions, and publications on these processes, including a handbook on the subject published by ASCD, are readily available (McCune 1986). Suffice it to point out that the process is fundamental to SBM.

Sample Policy 5

The board of education will annually review the mission statement of the district and select goals for the coming year.

Sample Policy 6

Building principals will annually report to the superintendent and the board of education their buildings' progress in reaching their goals, and they will explain how these accomplishments contribute to district goals.

Sample Regulation 6.1. Building principals, having been informed of the district goals, will submit objectives for their buildings with plans for their accomplishment.

Goal setting is easier to talk about than to do. The classic method of arriving at goals is through identifying needs, or by comparing what is with what should be. Because there are likely to be more needs or gaps than there can be goals in any given time frame, planners must set priorities. But if an organization deals only with priorities, it runs the risk of neglecting ongoing or routine needs. The sensible response to this dilemna is to select areas of emphasis for a given year carefully, while also maintaining attention to continuing goals that can never be abandoned.

The struggles involved in goal setting nurture the growth of all concerned and deepen their understanding of the relationships among specific objectives, broad goals, and the institutional mission. Figure 2 shows a forced-planning management model, so named because planning is a management function that should be continuous, rather than done at stated intervals. Moreover, planning that does not become operationalized is often useless. A management model that everyone in the organization understands and uses promotes the viability of SBM. The model in Figure 2 underscores the importance of developing and using a database, as discussed in the section "Information Sharing."

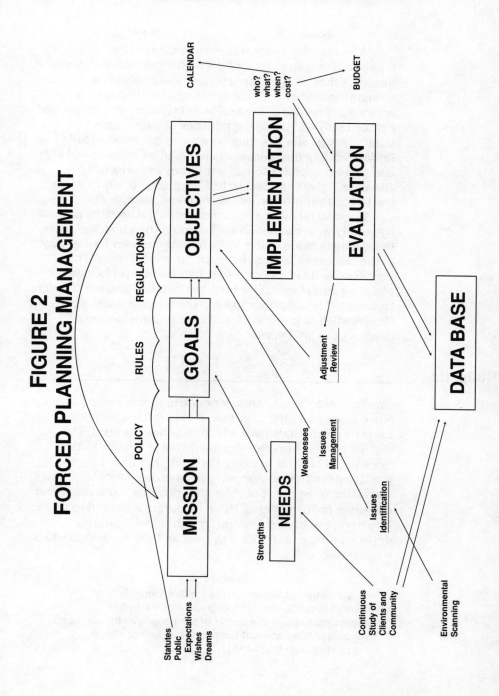

FIGURE 2
FORCED PLANNING MANAGEMENT

When setting goals, it is easy to fall into the tunnel-vision trap of adopting a highly mechanistic, linear model. Although such models have the appeal of a straightforward and logical approach, they ignore the nonrational nature of the real world (Patterson, Purkey, and Parker 1986) and the idiosyncracies of individuals. Inflexibility in process runs counter to the spirit of SBM. Understanding the "garbage can model" (Cohen et al. 1972) and accepting educational institutions as "organized anarchies" gives comfort to SBM enthusiasts who may be frustrated that it does not fall into neat packages.

The central office can facilitate the goal-setting process by supplying a simple format for submitting building plans. Budgeting is made easier if the format includes a summary of the resources needed for each planned activity. The process can be elaborated to provide a comprehensive planning model useful for both the building and the district. However, it is important to keep the arrangements simple. Proliferation of paperwork and bureaucratic process destroys the SBM spirit.

Budgeting

The crux of SBM is to transfer control to school buildings. Since money so often controls, it follows that buildings must be given funds over which they have control. The district budget provides the most visible answer to the question of how far to carry the SBM principle. The gradations of that answer vary from giving school buildings discretion over a part of their supply budget to giving them complete control over all fiscal resources assigned to them. The degree of budget control by individual buildings depends on the district's purposes and the context in which it operates.

Sample Policy 7

The annual budget of the Pleasant Valley School District is made up of the aggregate of those funds necessary to meet the needs of the programs in individual schools plus an amount needed for a central site to support building activities.

Although the suggested policy seems only to state the obvious, it does establish that specific amounts are budgeted for each building, setting a tone and suggesting a format for SBM. The sample policy also suggests abandonment of budgeting by a dollars-per-pupil formula in favor of allocations by objectives or programs.

There are two aspects to the budgeting process: One deals with determining the means by which funds are allocated, and the other deals with control of the allocation.

It is inconsistent with the tenets of SBM simply to allocate all buildings a prorated share of available funds. SBM assumes a difference in needs among buildings. The necessity, therefore, is to identify these variables among buildings that affect the amount of money each building needs to meet the needs of its students in keeping with district goals. The result will be variable allocations to the buildings. However, a sense of equity must be built into the process to achieve fair results. Discussion and eventual decision on an equitable allocation system is an excellent example of the kind of issue best solved by the principals' council. In any event, feelings that the allocation process is capricious or shows favoritism will quickly damage the trust level so important for successful SBM. A group process to determine the allocation system ensures its fairness and acceptance and also broadens understanding of the participants.

Sample Regulation 7.1. Funds for staffing school buildings will be allocated on the basis of number and type of students to be served.

Sample Regulation 7.2. Funds for the care and maintenance of school buildings and grounds will be allocated on the basis of the size, age, and physical characteristics of each building.

Staffing procedures are detailed in the next section of this book, "Allocating Personnel."

The operation, care, and maintenance of buildings frequently fall under central control, even in school districts deeply into SBM. Nevertheless, interesting opportunities are afforded when control is transferred to buildings. The School staff might care for a building so that less custodial time is needed if they are assured that the savings generated could be used to buy more instructional equipment. Teachers might turn off unused lights more frequently if the savings in the electrical bill would buy more books. Centralized maintenance systems are frequently a source of staff discontent, especially when things that need fixing are ignored while routine maintenance schedules go forward regardless of need. Certainly a sense of ownership will be developed by applying SBM principles to this aspect of school operation, resulting in better and less expensive care of buildings.

The implementation problem is twofold: Developing an allocation system for building maintenance is complex, and school staffs are outside their area of expertise in knowing when and how much service they need. Again, the principals' council is helpful in developing an allocation formula. Acceptable formulas are not impossible to develop. Many are already in place in the form of guidelines that central office staff use to make maintenance decisions in centralized management programs.

Principals may choose to keep the care of physical facilities primarily a central office function. Such a decision may be wise, but having the opportunity to make the decision is of psychological importance. Much of the feeling of powerlessness that prevails among building staffs is related to the relatively minor question of control over the maintenance system. A readily apparent limitation, however, is that SBM plans must include minimum standards of maintenance and periodic inspections by outside experts to protect against building deterioration.

Sample Policy 8

Budgeting and accounting procedures in the Pleasant Valley School District will provide for fiscal control at the school building level and flexibility in the use of funds.

Sample Regulation 8.1. The accounting system will establish each school site as a cost center having an annual appropriation. Monies expended at or for the school site will be charged against its appropriation.

Sample Regulation 8.2. Transfer of funds within accounts is permissible at the building level at the discretion of the building principal, provided that a summary of all such transfers is included in the principal's annual report.

Sample Regulation 8.3. Unspent funds in a school building appropriation at the end of any budget year are carried forward and added to the allocation for that building in the ensuing year. Allocations for the next year shall not be reduced on the basis of availability of carryover funds.

Requirements that all funds be spent within a given budget year—a common feature in handling public money—remove an important element of control. The need to get rid of money so as not to lose it hardly makes for judicious expenditures. SBM provides real ability to control an account over a period of time. Staff members are powerfully motivated when they can see the advantages in their own building of economies they make. Without SBM, economies attained in one building are often used to fund the extravagance of a neighboring building.

Implementing these concepts requires a change from conventional school accounting practices. Budget formats and accounting systems are frequently established by state statutes or other regulations. Because such regulations are easy to hide behind when the motive is to resist change, SBM managers must be creative. Identical budgets may need to be kept in two forms: one to fit state reporting requirements, and a duplicate transposed to workable SBM format. The SBM version will be by cost-center breakdowns and program-budgeting format. Willingness to adjust accounting to accommodate SBM is an important test of commitment.

If staff members are to participate in decisions that have the potential to maximize the usefulness of their dollars, they must understand the accounting system and have continuous access to the state of their accounts. Unfortunately, the practices used to account for public funds in federal, state, and local agencies seldom provide clear and current figures of fiscal position. School districts inherit many of these accounting problems. Nevertheless, school fiscal managers must aggressively seek simplified accounting procedures to implement SBM. Business establishments, because they price products and because they have more direct control, may offer valuable advice and useful models.

The concept that an expenditure at or for a building is charged to that building's account seems simple enough, but some twists in implementation affect SBM. For example, when a central office service is provided to a school, the method of cost determination can vary. On the one hand, the charge may be computed as the cost of materials and labor plus an overhead charge representing the cost of operating the central office. On the other hand, the charge may be materials and labor only, with costs of operating the central office paid with central office funds. Purists will argue that true cost must include an overhead, even including a portion of the superintendent's salary. Yet such computations cloud rather than simplify accounting from the building point of view. They also diminish site control, since site staff can't dictate the overhead cost. A suggested regulation for SBM purposes would be:

> *Sample Regulation 8.4.* Only direct costs will be charged against building appropriations for services provided by the central office. Overhead cost will be charged against the appropriations to the central office.

Carried to its ultimate, SBM would give the authority to individual buildings to contract for services with agencies other than the central office. Such a system would force the central office to be competitive in speed and cost. A recent *Fortune* magazine article (Pare' 1989) suggests that dramatic savings can accrue to businesses by forcing their central office staffs to compete with outside suppliers. If this route is chosen, the central office would obviously appreciate not having to charge for overhead; but its actual overhead would increase if the volume of its work diminished. The advantages of freedom for a building staff in these matters need to be balanced against the time and energy it takes them to micromanage business affairs as opposed to spending their time on instructional matters.

There is no recommendation implicit in this discussion. The purpose is to explore the variety of avenues SBM can follow and to emphasize that districts have alternatives from which to choose in installing SBM. One suspects that having the additional power is more a psychological than a real gain, and that in the business arena many principals will use less power than they are given.

Allocating Personnel

In terms of personnel, the implementation of SBM requires decisions about allocating, selecting, supervising, and developing staff, as well as administering staff contracts and keeping staff records.

A regulation was suggested earlier for the allocation of staff (see Sample Regulation 7.1). One mechanism for implementing the regulation is to provide a number of staffing points for each building. The points are spent by the building in selecting the number and type of staff desired. The points to be allocated are assigned to represent building needs; the points to be expended are related to salary requirements of the type of personnel requested. This system serves two purposes: It provides a way to allocate staff that is equitable for all buildings, and it lets each building control the configuration of staff to meet its needs. See Figure 3 for an example of point allocation.

Assume an elementary school of 362 full-time students, 72 of whom are on free lunch, 18 level I handicapped, 3 level II handicapped, 2 level III handicapped, and 22 gifted. The building is allocated 426 staffing points, including 7.6 for

FIGURE 3
SAMPLE POINT-ALLOCATION TABLE

Schools Receive Points:		Schools Are Charged Points:	
1	per student additionally:	22	per assistant principal
.2	per free lunch student	20	per team leader
1	per level I handicapped	20	per department chair
2	per level II handicapped	18	per classroom teacher
3	per level III handicapped	20	per specialist (4 per day)
.5	per gifted student	19	per librarian
.2	per each student less than 400	19	per counselor
1	per each mobility percentage point	8	per office worker (8 hr.)
		6	per aide (6 hr.)
		8	per custodian (8 hr.)

being less than optimum size and 6 for having a 6-percent mobility rate. The reason for allocating points on the basis of student mobility is that a high rate of student transfers increases student need and staff load. The rationale for giving extra points to small schools is to compensate them for the flexibility enjoyed by larger schools and to recognize the need for certain staff categories, regardless of school size. Librarians, for example, are not directly related to enrollment.

Librarians and counselors in this sample cost more points on the assumption that their certification is at the masters' degree level. Specialists in this sample are special education teachers, some of whom may be itinerant.

As illustrated in Figure 4, School A, in a team-teaching mode, has chosen to have three teams. Each team is staffed with a team leader, 4 teachers, and 2 aides, and serves 121

FIGURE 4
SAMPLE APPLICATION OF USE

Cost In Points	Staff Category	School A Staff Number	School A Points Charged	School B Staff Number	School B Points Charged	School C Staff Number	School C Points Charged	School D Staff Number	School D Points Charged
22	Assistant principal								
20	Team leader	3	60	3	60				
18	Classroom teacher	12	216	15	270	21	378	14	252
20	Specialist	2	40	1	20	415	16	2	40
19	Counselor	1	19						
19	Librarian	1	19	1	19			1	19
8	Office worker	1	8	2	16	2	16	1	8
6	Teacher aide	8	48	4	24			15	90
8	Custodian	2	16	2	16	2	16	2	16
	Totals		426		425		426		425

students. The teams are supported by 2 specialists, each of whom has an aide. A counselor, a librarian, and one office clerk complete the staffing for School A.

School B, also a team-teaching school, has chosen to have a richer teacher-student ratio at the team level. Each of its three teams is staffed with a team leader, 5 teachers, and 1 aide per 121 students. The teams are supported by just one specialist, a librarian, and two office workers, but no counselor.

School C, organized on a self-contained classroom basis, wants to provide the smallest class size possible. Its staffing configuration provides an average class size of 17.2 students, but very little support.

School D, also self-contained, has an average class size of 25.8 students, but all teachers, including the specialists, have their own aides.

It must be noted that, although the cost of a category of employees in terms of staffing points must bear a relationship to the salary paid, it cannot be a straight line relationship to the salary of each individual employee. Salary schedules frequently pay experienced teachers twice as much as beginners. Formulas that encourage or allow a building to trade two beginning teachers for one veteran are questionable and certainly would not endear SBM to the leaders in the profession.

As in other aspects of SBM, a decision must be made regarding how far to go with the plan. At one extreme, all staff members except the principal are included in the formula. Indeed, the Hill City School in Hill City, Minnesota, does not have a principal but is operated solely by teachers, with some supervision from the district superintendent (National Clearinghouse on School-Based Management 1989). Gradations of the plan keep some types of employees outside the system to ensure minimum or standard staffing levels for some functions. Interesting questions arise. For example, if custodians are part of the formula, can a building staff agree that each staff member will share some cleaning duties, eliminating the need for custodians? Can a building be allowed to have no certified librarian, no school nursing services, or no specialized counseling services?

Obviously, maximum flexibility has the potential to run afoul of union contracts, state and accreditation association regulations, and the interests of certain employee groups. The dilemma is that if too many staff categories fall outside the formula, control and flexibility of the building are diminished. The problems are real and severe. As is so often the case when trying to implement SBM, meaningful struggles expose the sacred cows in our accepted practices and force practical solutions to ambiguous, theoretical questions. The stiff back of bureaucracy will not be broken until the real issues are attacked.

Allowing for the selection of staff at the building level is a fairly easy mechanism to put in place.

Sample Policy 9
The selection of staff assigned to a school building will be made by the building principal, subject to the approval of the board of education.

Although final selection may be deferred to the principal, a great deal of service can be provided a building by a central human resources office. The details associated with recruiting, checking applications, and following up on recommendations are time consuming and require experience and expertise.

Sample Regulation 9.1. The human resources office of the Pleasant Valley School District is responsible for initial screening of all applicants for employment and for keeping a current list of all candidates meeting district standards for employability. Principals will recommend staff from the approved list to fill their buildings' vacancies.

Decisions also must be made regarding the degree of staff or constituent involvement in staff selection. This decision will vary depending on the staff category being filled. Selection of a part-time food-service worker differs from selection of an assistant principal. The procedure used is less important than the requirement that all staff members understand the procedure and the extent of their involvement in advance.

A common procedure establishes a committee charged with defining the criteria that guide the appointment. If the committee is only to establish criteria, as compared with making an actual selection, it is important that they understand this limitation. If the committee is to make a selection, how that selection is to be made should be understood in advance. Plurality vote is different from consensus; weighting prioritized lists can produce different results from votes on single candidates. Some SBM plans have elaborate written agreements between the central office and buildings and between buildings and SBM management teams. These are useful in clarifying roles, responsibilities, and limitations of all those involved in staff selection. The caution for such instruments is that their detail may move school districts into varying levels of additional bureaucracy or inflexibility, and that they may suggest a standardized model that invites uniformity.

Suggestions for supervising personnel were provided in the chapter, "Define New Leadership Roles." A sample procedure for putting these ideas into practice deemphasizes much of the current attention to evaluating staff performance. In keeping with the concept of management by exception, the principal is not required to turn in an annual or routine evaluation for each staff member. Instead, the principal is expected to inform the central office of those individuals whose performance is marginal and for whom she is developing specific plans for improvement or assembling documentation that could lead to dismissal.

The rationale for this procedure is the assumption that SBM staffs are collaborating on the improvement of practices to help students learn. This assumption includes the notion that real teaching improvement occurs when teachers work together toward achieving building-level instructional goals. The corollary assumption is that traditional evaluation processes that deal individually with each teacher tend to be demeaning, concentrate on individual as opposed to group improvement, have the potential for destroying collegial relationships, breed apprehension and mistrust, inhibit risk taking and innovation, and take an inordinate amount of the principal's time.

Rather than looking for better evaluation instruments, leaders interested in SBM should consider carefully the results achieved by the time spent on formal teacher procedures.

The management of human resources in any institution has become quite complex. The management of fringe benefit packages, along with the record keeping involved in sick leave, progressions on salary schedules, health insurance, and so on, are examples of personnel activities better handled centrally. Adding these chores at the building level would not increase school-level control; doing them centrally provides a valuable service. The objective is to strike an appropriate balance in this respect and to reserve time and effort at the building level for attention to staff development activities that improve instruction.

Sample Regulation 9.2. The human resources office of the Pleasant Valley School District is responsible for managing all contracts made with employee organizations and for keeping current and accurate personnel records for all district employees.

Activities of school personnel are restricted by many regulations, some of which arise from district rules, some from union contracts, and others from state regulations. SBM is enhanced when principals are allowed as much flexibility as possible in enforcement of regulations.

Sample Regulation 9.3. Principals have the responsibility, within district guidelines, for setting opening and closing times at their school buildings, including hours of in-building work for staff.

Teachers are quick to notice perceived inequalities from one building to another in hours of work. Union contracts often exact rigid uniformity on such matters. Nevertheless, it is precisely this lack of control that gives teachers a feeling of powerlessness. Successful implementation of SBM sometimes requires running the risks of potential abuse to gain the advantages of empowerment. Put more positively, SBM makes creative noncompliance unnecessary. A statement of the Riverside, California, Unified District (Lantz n.d.), says it well: "The organization should avoid imposing general rules and regulations designed to protect against mistakes because such rules and regulations tend to be designed with the least competent individuals in mind, and uniform application of those rules will tend to force all individuals to

perform uniformly at the lowest common level of
performance."

Establishing Curriculum

The greatest opportunities for achieving the overriding
objective of SBM—better learning for students—are in the
areas of curriculum and instruction. Although the broad
outlines of curriculum content may be set by external
forces, teacher attention to its scope and sequence,
articulation, alignment with the testing program, and
assessment are indispensable to success.

There are good reasons for a degree of standardization
of the content of curriculum. The rate of student movement
from school to school (20 percent per year by some
estimates) argues for some standardization. Competence in
the basic skills is a universal requirement. And overall
results—the basis for determining the success of SBM—will
be judged in terms of a fairly standard curriculum. Evidence
that this is true can be found in results of a recent Phi Delta
Kappa Gallup Poll (Elam and Gallup September 1989)
showing that most respondents favored a national
curriculum. Thus, in a general sense, curriculum content is
standardized by external forces.

Still, SBM can give building staffs maximum flexibility to
select and to experiment with teaching methods and can
permit them to match curriculum with student needs.
Selection of textbooks and materials, arrangement of
instructional time, appropriate use of field trips, articulation
of materials among and within grade levels and integration
of homework or schoolwide projects are all examples of
instructional decisions reserved completely to the building.

One implementation hurdle that SBM must overcome is
the habit of some school boards of extending their
authority beyond the policy level and into areas of
judgment best left to professionals.

Sample Policy 10
The role of the Pleasant Valley Board of Education with
regard to instruction is to approve goals and monitor
results. The arrangement of curriculum content and the

selection of methods and materials is delegated to the staff.

Selection of textbooks is a district function in many school districts and a state function in others. A significant advantage of districtwide selection is the staff development support that can more easily be provided when the entire district is using the same materials. Some cost savings may also be realized in bulk purchases, and a greater depth of expertise is afforded the selection process when it is done centrally. Nevertheless, freedom to select their own materials empowers teachers in a visible and meaningful way.

Sample Regulation 10.1. Building principals, in consultation with their instructional staffs, will select the instructional materials used in their buildings.

To take advantage of the savings and expertise inherent in central textbook selection without denying the buildings some degree of control, an alternative position is possible:

Sample Alternative Regulation 10.1. In the Pleasant Valley School District, the central office will adopt a list of textbooks and will support their use throughout the district. School buildings wishing to depart from the district adoption may do so with the approval of the superintendent.

Decision Making

A persistent problem in any complex organization is the difficulty individuals have in recognizing how and when they influence decisions. Human nature dictates that people tend to feel uninvolved or ignored when they disagree with the final outcome of a decision. It is extremely important, therefore, for SBM leadership to expose the decision-making process as clearly as possible and to follow it faithfully to maintain the trust and ownership necessary for successful SBM.

A useful way to clarify decision making is by developing a matrix. In its simplest form, a matrix lists the staff members involved on one axis, lists the activities on a second axis, and provides a set of codes to describe the degree of involvement of each member in a given activity.

The sample matrix in Figure 5 shows how decisions are made in the Pleasant Valley School District regarding the purchase of instructional equipment.

Although a matrix may identify individual responsibility for decisions, much of the SBM philosophy holds that decision making is a group process. Identifying

FIGURE 5
DECISION-MAKING MATRIX

Pleasant Valley School District
Program for Equipping Schools

	Setting Goals for Program	Budgeting for Program	Allocating Budget	Writing Specifications	Taking Bids and Purchasing	Accounting and Inventory	Evaluating Program
Board of education	A	A			A		
Superintendent	R	R	A				A
Principal's council	r	r	R	r			R
Principal	r		r	r			r
Teacher or user	r		r	r			r
Subject matter consultant	r	r	r	r			r
Business manager	r	r	r	A	r	R	r
Purchasing agent				D	D		r
Accountant						A	r

A	=	Authority to act
D	=	Delegated authority to act
R	=	Major responsibility for initiating recommendation
r	=	May recommend; should be consulted

decision-making groups and defining their functions are important. In many SBM plans, the core decision-making group is the school council, which is often known by other names but is generally the representative group responsible for school improvement. Central task forces or planning councils are also common in the installation of SBM. The North Syracuse, New York, Central School District has a simple, clear diagram that illustrates the relationships among these groups (Figure 6).

The decision-making tree, popular in business and industry, is another device for clarifying how decisions are made. It's important not to prescribe implementing mechanisms but, rather, to emphasize staff understanding of the decision-making process. For a useful model applicable to the school-level decision-making process, see *How to Make Decisions That Stay Made* (Saphier, Bigda-Peyton, and Pierson 1989).

Information Sharing

Knowledge is power. To withhold information is an act of preserving rather than sharing power. The successful implementation of SBM, therefore, depends on finding effective ways to collect needed information and to distribute salient information to the entire staff. Because of the huge amount of information available, the problem is not just to collect and disseminate it, but also to sort the available information to determine what is useful, as well as to arrange and present it in ways that make it understandable.

A promising way to implement this phase of SBM is the development of a management information system (MIS). The purpose of such a system is to define the information needed, to provide for its efficient collection, to arrange it for easy interpretation, and to find suitable ways to share it. Sites are best served when the MIS is organized as a central office service, provided that its purposes are clearly defined to maximize the easy flow of information. The emerging business model places a person designated as the MIS officer in the highest level of the corporate structure.

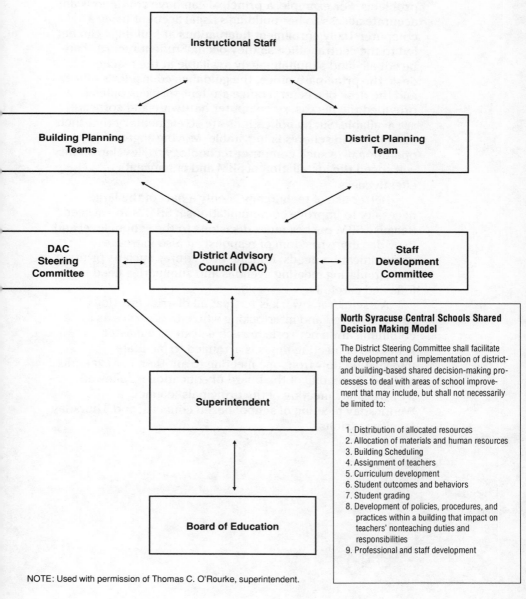

FIGURE 6
PLANNING COUNCIL DIAGRAM

**North Syracuse Central School District
Shared Decision-Making Model**

Instructional Staff

Building Planning Teams

District Planning Team

DAC Steering Committee

District Advisory Council (DAC)

Staff Development Committee

Superintendent

Board of Education

North Syracuse Central Schools Shared Decision Making Model

The District Steering Committee shall facilitate the development and implementation of district- and building-based shared decision-making processess to deal with areas of school improvement that may include, but shall not necessarily be limited to:

1. Distribution of allocated resources
2. Allocation of materials and human resources
3. Building Scheduling
4. Assignment of teachers
5. Curriculum development
6. Student outcomes and behaviors
7. Student grading
8. Development of policies, procedures, and practices within a building that impact on teachers' nonteaching duties and responsibilities
9. Professional and staff development

NOTE: Used with permission of Thomas C. O'Rourke, superintendent.

51

Establishment of an MIS is enabled by the intelligent application of computer technology. An integrated computer system that provides every building instant access to the MIS is technically feasible and solves many problems. For example, a principal can have continuous and accurate access to her building's fiscal account using a computer. Daily enrollment fluctuations at buildings can be fed to the central office as they occur. Student records can be equally and simultaneously available at the teacher's desk, the principal's office, the guidance counselor's office, and the desk of a central office student-services official, provided the necessary computer hardware and software are available. Such applications are so elementary that their installation in schools is inevitable. Moving aggressively to operationalize such computer technology to develop an MIS will speed the installation of SBM and enhance its effectiveness.

Better use of technology is only a part of the larger necessity to improve communications if SBM is to succeed. Because SBM pushes more decisions to the school level and provides more freedom of response, it also increases communication needs. Routine procedures such as printing and circulating meeting agendas and summaries need to be followed carefully.

A useful framework is to treat all district meetings as a connected and interlocking whole that serves as a communication network. In such a system, a master schedule of meeting times is arranged to facilitate information flow from one meeting to another. For example, a Monday meeting of the board of education is followed by a Tuesday meeting of the principals' council, a Wednesday meeting of school-based councils, and Thursday faculty sessions.

A Reflective Postscript

In a Philosophic Rather Than a Practical Vein, One Marvels
at the apparent inconsistencies in trends to which
educators must respond. Witness the long-uninterrupted
centralizing trend from the family-controlled schools of the
original colonies to the highly organized bureaucracies of
today. The growth of state departments of education, the
gradual move to aggressive federal participation, and,
finally, a national summit to set educational goals are all
examples of centralizing pressures. School boards, whose
formation was a centralizing move itself, complain of the
erosion of their role through legislative action, more
frequent litigation, and growth of collective employee
strength.

Recognition that these societal changes are driven by
advancing technology and economic globalization does not
provide much assurance of reversal. Does the call for SBM
at this juncture in history pull educational leadership in
opposite directions?

Perhaps not, if faith in SBM springs from a conviction
that it is a necessary and important accommodation to
the growing complexity of society. SBM takes full account
of the human element in complex organizations. It prevents
the failures that arise from bureaucratic overload and
impersonality. Seen in this light, SBM neither reverses
trends nor stands in the way of progress, but becomes the
indispensable ingredient by which more complex
organizations succeed.

I have said very little here about relationships with
teacher associations or unions as part of the process of
installing SBM. Not much need be said of the evident
requirement for cooperation. Currently, there seems to be
no problem as unions appear to enthusiastically embrace
SBM—and to demand some form of it. There is little

evidence that union leadership views SBM as threatening and little concern that some of the freedom needed for full implementation requires unions, as well as administrations, to give up power. We can hope that unions will continue to support SBM, but in some cases they may not.

A recent *Wall Street Journal* article (Koenig 1990) refers to a comparable concern in the industrial sector. The story describes the successful challenge of the Chemical Workers Association to a quality-circle design team formed by the Dupont Company. Although quality circles are a revered form of moving decisions closer to the point of implementation and are generally lauded by both labor and management, an administrative law judge ruled that in the DuPont case, the design team violated federal labor law. This dispute demonstrates the potential for implementation of SBM to threaten union power.

Consider an example of ultimate SBM implementation in which the entire salary appropriation is turned over to a building to manage. The building staff, responding to the law of supply and demand, may decide that having a good science teacher in the building is reason enough to pay a higher salary on the basis of subject matter. A building staff seriously committed to the improvement of learning for students may agree to make some sacrifices to achieve an important instructional objective. Whatever flexibility SBM provides for managing the salary budget threatens the stability and importance of a negotiated salary schedule. Yet without the flexibility to make the changes to which the staff agrees, there is no reason to give them site-based control.

A number of similar scenarios can be developed to show that the farther down the SBM path a district travels, the more union power is diluted. In a sense, the negotiating process depends on and assumes central control for the negotiated contract to have force and meaning. One may argue that the negotiations to protect employees can move to the site as SBM is implemented. This argument loses strength, however, when one considers the nature of the relationships at the building level envisioned for successful SBM.

To the credit of union leadership, no one to date has accused boards of education or administrators of using SBM as a union-breaking device. Happily, all sides are cloaked in the pious declarations that the motivation for SBM is to help students learn. Fortunately, installation of SBM processes appears to foster collaboration rather than confrontation. And as long as that trend prevails, we can chalk up a huge benefit from SBM.

The issue is raised here only to alert those interested in SBM of a latent problem as the concept advances and if unions become threatened. Empowering teachers is not the same as providing more power to unions.

Finally, it must be emphasized that SBM cannot be successful in the absence of a huge element of trust. SBM is a process, not a product. Moreover, it is a continuing process that can be implemented in many ways and to differing degrees. It is an ongoing process in the sense that most school districts already have some elements of SBM in place. This book is intended to help them accelerate the process of SBM implementation.

References and Resources

References

American Association of School Administrators. (March 15, 1990). *Leadership News* 61: 3.

Boyer, E. (August 1989). "School Reform Needs National Focus." *The School Administrator* 46, 7: 48.

Bradley, A. (May 9, 1990). "New York City Schools Take First Step Toward Management at the School Site." *Education Week* 9, 33: 5.

Burns, L., and J. Howes. (August 1988). "Handing Control to Local Schools." *The School Administrator* 45, 7: 8-10.

Carr, R. (August 1988). "Second Wave Reforms Crest at Local Initiative." *The School Administrator* 45, 7: 16-18.

Cohen, M. (1988). *Restructuring the Educational System: Agenda for the 1990s*. Washington, D.C.: National Governors' Association, Center for Policy Research.

Cohen, M., J. March, and J. Olsen. (March 1972). "A Garbage Can Model of Organizational Choice." *Administrative Science Quarterly* 17, 1: 1-25.

Elam, S.M., and A.M. Gallup. (September 1989). "The 21st Annual Gallup Poll." *Kappan* 71, 1: 41-54.

Fulbright, L. (October 30, 1989). "School-Centered Decision-Making Comes to Light: Site-Based Management Renamed." *AASA Leadership News* 54.

Hansen, B.J., and C.L. Marburger. (1988). *School Based Improvement: A Manual for District Leaders*. Columbia, Md.: National Committee for Citizens in Education.

Koenig, R. (March 28, 1990). "Quality Circles Are Vulnerable to Union Tests." *Wall Street Journal* B1.

Lantz, G.C. (n.d.) "Riverside Unified District: Participation Management System." (Unpublished report, Riverside, Calif.)

Marburger, C.L. (1985). *One School at a Time*. Columbia, Md.: National Committee for Citizens in Education.

McCune, S. (1986). *Guide to Strategic Planning for Educators*. Alexandria, Va.: Association for Supervision and Curriculum Development.

Mitchell, J.E. (February 1990). "Coaxing Staff from Cages for Site-Based Decisions to Fly." *The School Administrator* 47, 2: 23-29.

Murphy, J. (June 1989). "The Paradox of Decentralizing Schools: Lesson from Business, Government and the Catholic Church." *Kappan* 70, 10: 808-812.

National Clearinghouse on School Based Management. (1989). *School Based Management Forum*. Westbury, N.Y.: The Institute for Advancing Educational Management.

Paré, T.E. (September 11, 1989). "How to Cut the Cost of Headquarters." *Fortune*, 189-196.

Patterson, J.L., S.C. Purkey, and J.V. Parker. (1986). *Productive School Systems for a Nonrational World*. Alexandria, Va.: Association for Supervision and Curriculum Development.

Pierce, N.R. (September 3, 1989). "Educational Summit Good But Just First Step." Lincoln, Nebraska, *Sunday Journal Star*.

Saphier, J., T. Bigda-Peyton, and G. Pierson. (1989). *How to Make Decisions That Stay Made*. Alexandria, Va.: Association for Supervision and Curriculum Development.

Snider, W. (October 25, 1989). "Cavazos Couples Parental Choice, Site Management." *Education Week*, 1.

Snider, W. (March 14, 1990). "Chicago Councils Begin to Decide Fate of Principals." *Education Week* 9, 25: 1, 13.

Weick, K. (March 1976). "Educational Organizations as Loosely Coupled Systems." *Administrative Science Quarterly* 21, 1: 1-19.

White, P.A. (September 1989). "An Overview of School Based Management: What Does Research Say?" *NASSP Bulletin* 73, 518: 1-7.

Woodward, J. (1958). *Management and Technology*. London: Her Majesty's Stationery Office.

Additional Resources

Blumberg, A., and W. Greenfield. (1980). *The Effective Principal: Perspectives on School Leadership*. Boston: Allyn & Bacon.

Brandt, R.S. (May 1989). "On Teacher Empowerment: A Conversation with Ann Lieberman." *Educational Leadership* 46, 8: 23-26.

Floden, R.E., A.C. Porter, L.E. Alford, D.J. Freeman, S. Irwin, W.H. Schmidt, and J.R. Schwille. (May 1989). "Instructional Leadership at the District Level: A Closer Look at Autonomy and Control." *Educational Administration Quarterly* 24, 2: 96-121.

Fulbright, L., ed. (1988). *School Based Management: A Strategy for Better Learning*. Washington, D.C.: American Association of School Administrators, National Association of Secondary School Principals, and National Association of Elementary School Principals.

Kaestle, C.F., and M.S. Smith. (November 1982). "The Federal Role in Elementary and Secondary Education." *Harvard Educational Review* 52, 4: 384-408.

Lewis, A. (1989). *Restructuring America's Schools*.Arlington, Va.: American Association of School Administrators.

Lieberman, A. (May 1988). "Teachers and Principals: Turf, Tension and New Tasks." *Kappan* 69, 9: 648-653.

Malen, B., R.T. Ogawa, and J. Kranz. (February 1990). "Site-Based Management: Unfulfilled Promises." *The School Administrator* 47, 2: 30, 53-59.

Phillips, P.R. (March 1989). "Shared Decision Making in an Age of Reform." *Updating School Board Policies* 20, 3: 1-5.

Prele, P.K., and S.C. Smith, eds. (1989). *School Leadership Handbook for Excellence*. 2d ed. Eugene, Ore.: ERIC

Clearinghouse on Educational Management. College of
Education, University of Oregon.

Sasse, C., ed. (1989). *Restructuring Education: What It Means
for Principals*. Tallahassee, Fla.: Florida Department of
Education, Office of Policy Research and Improvement.

White, P.A. (1988). *Resource Material on School Based
Management*. New Brunswick, N.J.: Center for Policy
Research in Education, Eagleton Institute, Rutgers
University.